THE KING

THE ROYAL & THE SERVANT

BY JON ROBERT QUINN

Chapter 1 Page 9

Kingdom's Blueprint

Chapter 2 Page 22

King's Throne: The Owner's Realm

Chapter 3 Page 36

Royal's Crown: Leadership and Stability

Chapter 4 Page 51

Servant's Path: Struggles of the Working Class

Chapter 5 Page 65

Kingdom's Economy: Wealth Distribution and Power

Chapter 6 Page 81

Royal Dilemma: Balancing Leadership & Compassion

Chapter 7 Page 97

Servant's Drive: Overcoming Financial Struggles

Chapter 8 Page 113

King's Legacy: Creating a Sustainable Kingdom

Chapter 9 Page 128

Unity in the Kingdom: A Balanced Economy

Chapter 10 Page 143

Kingdom's Future: Building a Legacy for Generations

Foreword

A number of years ago, I had the privilege of meeting Mark, the owner of a local gas station chain. At the time, he owned about 15 to 20 Arco gas stations. If you value each station at around $5 million—quite a conservative estimate—we're talking about a net worth of roughly $100 million. That isn't chump change. Yet, what struck me most during that conversation wasn't the wealth Mark had accumulated but something far more profound.

We were talking about the people who worked at his stations when I mentioned how polite and friendly the lady behind the counter was. Mark smiled and nodded, sharing that she was one of his regular cashiers. I asked him why he hadn't promoted her to manager, to which he replied, "She's happy where she is." And with that simple statement, Mark introduced me to the concept of The King, The Royal, and The Servant.

Mark explained how each person in his business was playing an essential role, not just in terms of the station's daily operations, but in terms of their place in the broader world. The King, the Royal, and the Servant. The King is the owner, the visionary, the one who takes risks and creates an empire. The Royal is the leader, the manager, the one who ensures that the King's vision is executed day in and day out. And then there's the Servant—the worker, the one who performs the essential tasks that keep the system running.

I was struck by how simple and yet profound this thinking was. Mark wasn't just talking about a hierarchy in business; he was describing a philosophy for life. It made me realize that while not everyone aspires to be the King or the Royal, that doesn't diminish the importance of the Servant. There's value in every role, and each person contributes to the success of the whole. For the first time, I understood that it's not just about financial success or power—it's about understanding where you are and what role you play in the larger system.

That day changed my perspective on life and business. I've thought about The King, The Royal, and The Servant concept for over ten years now, often bringing it up in conversations and incorporating it into many of my books as an example. But I've never written an entire book about this philosophy—until now. After a decade of reflection and observation, I've come to see this concept reflected in almost every corner of my life. It's evident in business, in politics, in social structures—everywhere I look, I see these dynamics at play.

I realized it was time to share this thinking with the world in a more structured, purposeful way. The King, The Royal, and The Servant are more than just labels for positions in an organization; they represent a framework for understanding how societies, businesses, and even our own lives function. It's about knowing where you stand, what role you play, and how you can evolve from one role to the next.

In this book, I'll take you deeper into this philosophy. I'll explore how each role contributes to the whole, how these roles interrelate, and how anyone can move from one position to another through education, passion, dedication, and, sometimes, a bit of luck.

This is a concept that goes beyond business. It's a lens through which we can better understand not only organizations but the world itself.

I'm excited to finally share this philosophy with you. It's been a long time coming, but I believe it's a message worth spreading. Thank you for taking the time to explore this idea with me.

— Jon Robert Quinn

Chapter 1:

The Kingdom's Blueprint

In every kingdom, there are three essential elements that form the foundation of its operation. These roles—The King, The Royal, and The Servant—are not just arbitrary titles; they represent the pillars of any functioning society, organization, or business. Each of these roles plays an integral part in ensuring the success of the whole system. The King, the Royal, and the Servant may seem like vastly different figures, but their roles are interdependent, and together, they create the structure upon which prosperity is built.

In this chapter, we'll explore these three roles in depth, understanding not only what each represents but also how they interact with one another and how each contributes to the greater good of the kingdom. We'll delve into the realities of their positions, including the inherent challenges that come with them, and how they all play a crucial part in the success or failure of an organization. Additionally, we'll introduce the idea that in order for a society to run, all three roles are necessary—each fulfilling a distinct purpose that supports the others. Moreover, anyone can transition from one role to the next, but this journey requires more than just hard work or education alone. It takes a combination of passion, dedication, tenacity, skill, and sometimes, a bit of luck. Only then can one move upward from Servant to Royal, and from Royal to King.

The King: Visionary and Creator

At the top of the organizational hierarchy stands the King. The King is the creator, the visionary, the one who owns and risks everything to build an empire. This role is not simply about holding power or wealth —it is about the ability to see beyond the present and into the future. The King is often the one who has the initial idea, the one who dreams of what can be, even when others doubt the possibility. The King represents entrepreneurship, ambition, and the courage to venture into the unknown.

The King is the one who takes risks—sometimes calculated, sometimes gut-driven. They put everything they have on the line, often risking their personal wealth, reputation, and even relationships in pursuit of a dream. The King is not only a leader but a creator of systems, a builder of legacies. They are the ones who start businesses, create new products, and innovate. They are responsible for establishing the direction of the kingdom and setting the long-term vision that guides everything within it.

But with this great power comes an equally great burden. While the King enjoys the rewards of financial freedom, their success is not guaranteed. The King must also bear the responsibility for the failures. If the kingdom falters, the King alone is accountable. This weight is not easy to carry, but it is a responsibility that is rewarded by the freedom that comes with owning and controlling the empire. A successful King is financially independent—their wealth is generated by the success of the kingdom they have built. They have the ability to make choices that go beyond day-to-day survival. Financial freedom allows the King to invest in new ventures, take personal risks, and shape their future.

However, it is important to understand that financial freedom comes at a cost. The King's journey is often one of sacrifice. They may face long hours, difficult decisions, and high-stakes situations. They may sacrifice personal time and relationships in pursuit of their goals. The King's life is one of ambition, but it is also a life marked by isolation, uncertainty, and, often, personal sacrifice.

The Royal: The Leader Who Bridges the Gap

Below the King is the Royal—the leader who runs the day-to-day operations of the kingdom. The Royal is tasked with taking the King's vision and turning it into a reality. While the King is focused on the long-term, big-picture goals, the Royal is on the front lines, ensuring that the organization functions smoothly on a daily basis. The Royal is the one who implements strategy, manages resources, and ensures that everyone in the organization is working toward the same goal.

The Royal, unlike the King, does not own the kingdom. While they may be financially stable, they do not enjoy the ultimate financial freedom that the King experiences. The Royal's wealth and success are closely tied to their position within the organization. They are compensated for their leadership and management abilities, but they do not share the same level of financial independence that the King enjoys. The Royal is a leader, but their role is still very much defined by their relationship to the King and the broader organization.

Despite not holding the ultimate power, the Royal is a critical figure in the kingdom. The Royal is the one who manages people, keeps the operations running, and ensures that the goals of the organization are met. They act as the intermediary between the King and the Servants. The Royal is in a unique position to understand both the larger vision and the day-to-day realities of the kingdom. They are often the ones who deal with the practical issues that arise within the organization, ensuring that systems are functioning, people are motivated, and resources are being used efficiently.

The Royal faces their own set of challenges. They must balance the King's ambitions with the needs of the people they lead. They must maintain stability and ensure that the kingdom is profitable, all while managing the pressures of leadership. This delicate balance can be difficult to achieve. The Royal's ability to lead with both vision and practicality is what ultimately ensures the success of the kingdom.

The Servant: The Backbone of the Kingdom

While the King and Royal are often seen as the leaders, it is the Servant who forms the backbone of the kingdom. The Servants are the workers, the ones who do the everyday tasks that keep the kingdom functioning. They may be employees, laborers, or lower-level managers—each playing a critical role in the daily operations of the business. They are the ones who show up every day, perform their tasks, and ensure that the business keeps moving forward.

The Servant's role is often undervalued or underappreciated. They are the ones who toil day in and day out, doing the essential work that no one else wants to do. Despite their critical importance, Servants are often the least financially secure. While the King and the Royal enjoy financial freedom and stability, the Servant struggles to make ends meet. They often face financial hardship, living paycheck to paycheck, working long hours for a relatively low wage.

But the financial struggles of the Servant are not solely a result of a lack of effort or intelligence. Many Servants are incredibly hard-working and dedicated, but they often lack access to the same resources and opportunities that the King and Royal have. They may not have the education, the connections, or the financial backing to rise above their current situation. This is where the challenges of the kingdom become more evident. While the King enjoys the freedom of wealth, and the Royal enjoys stability, the Servant is left with the daily grind and the struggle to achieve financial security.

Yet, despite these challenges, the Servant is not without hope. The Servant plays a crucial role in the kingdom's success, and through education, dedication, and hard work, they can elevate their position. The Servant may rise to the Royal position through skill, knowledge, and leadership ability. And with enough ambition, drive, and sometimes a bit of luck, the Servant can transition into the King's role, gaining financial freedom and the ability to create their own empire.

The Interdependence of the King, the Royal, and the Servant

It is vital to understand that all three roles—the King, the Royal, and the Servant—are necessary for the success of the kingdom. A kingdom cannot function with just one of these roles. Each role supports the others, and without any one of them, the entire system would collapse. The King may have the vision and the financial freedom, but without the Royal to implement the vision and the Servants to do the work, the empire would never thrive. Similarly, the Royal would have no foundation without the Servants, and the Servants would have no opportunities without the King and the Royal to provide guidance and leadership.

While the King is the visionary, the Royal is the leader who brings that vision to life. And without the

Servants, neither the King nor the Royal would be able to achieve anything. It is through their combined efforts that the kingdom stands strong and grows.

The Journey from Servant to Royal to King

The most powerful idea in this framework is that anyone can move from one role to another. While the King, the Royal, and the Servant are often seen as fixed positions, the truth is that anyone, with the right mindset and dedication, can move up the ranks. The journey from Servant to Royal, or from Royal to King, requires more than just hard work. It requires a combination of education, passion, tenacity, skill, and luck. It takes an understanding that while hard work is crucial, it is not enough on its own. Education can help, but it too is not the sole factor in success.

Many Servants are hard-working and incredibly smart, yet they remain stuck in poverty due to circumstances beyond their control. The path upward requires more than just a strong work ethic or raw intelligence. It requires opportunities—education, connections, resources, and the willingness to learn and grow. Passion and dedication are also essential components in this journey. The Servant must be willing to take risks, push beyond their comfort zones, and actively seek ways to improve their situation.

In the end, the King, the Royal, and the Servant are not simply fixed roles—they are stepping stones. With the right mindset, anyone can transition from one role to the next, but it will take more than just effort. It will take a combination of key factors that align to create the right opportunity at the right time. The kingdom is not just a structure of wealth; it is a reflection of the potential within each person to rise to new heights.

Chapter 2:

The King's Throne: The Owner's Realm

At the apex of any successful organization stands the King—its owner, its creator, its visionary. The King is the one who builds the empire, who lays the foundation upon which all others stand. They command both the resources and the risks, controlling the direction of the business and determining its destiny. This is the role of the King: to see what others cannot, to take the bold steps that others are too hesitant to make, and to create something lasting and impactful. In the world of business, the King is the one who owns it all.

But the King's throne is not an easy one to occupy. The weight of that throne is heavy, and the responsibility it carries is immense. The King's success, their position of privilege, and their financial freedom come not from luck, but from years of hard work, sacrifices, and a relentless pursuit of growth and success. The King may sit at the top of the hierarchy, but the path to their throne is far from easy. In fact, the King's journey is one of constant struggle and decision-making. It is about more than just accumulating wealth; it's about maintaining control, pushing boundaries, and making tough choices, all while keeping an eye on the future.

The King's Privilege: Financial Freedom

The most obvious and perhaps the most celebrated aspect of the King's position is the financial freedom they hold. As the owner of a business or empire, the King has built something that grants them the freedom to live without the constant constraints of a paycheck. This freedom is what sets the King apart from others in the organization. It is the freedom to make decisions without the worry of financial instability. It is the freedom to invest, to risk, to explore new opportunities—all without the crushing weight of financial insecurity that so many others in the kingdom face.

For many, the concept of financial freedom is an abstract dream, something that seems unreachable. But for the King, it is a reality. The King has earned this privilege not by simply being handed wealth, but through years of hard work, smart decisions, and a clear understanding of the resources at their disposal. Financial freedom allows the King to make bold moves—investing in new ventures, hiring the right people, and expanding the business in ways that would be impossible for those living paycheck to paycheck.

Yet, while financial freedom is one of the King's greatest privileges, it also comes with its own set of challenges. The King does not sit comfortably in their wealth. Instead, they bear the constant weight of responsibility. Financial freedom does not mean the absence of risk; rather, it amplifies the stakes of every decision they make. With the wealth they control comes the responsibility to maintain and grow it. The King's financial position is not static—it requires constant management, strategic thinking, and sometimes, the willingness to take risks that could lead to great rewards or devastating losses.

The King's Responsibility: Risk and Decision-Making

Being a King is about more than just enjoying the fruits of success; it is about constantly managing risks and making decisions that will impact not only the future of the organization but the livelihoods of everyone involved. The King is responsible for the entire kingdom's success, including the roles of the Royal and the Servants, and must make decisions that can either propel the business forward or set it back.

The King's role is not one of comfort, despite what the position might suggest. The King's wealth is often tied to the success of the business, which means every decision they make carries significant weight. The King must constantly evaluate market conditions, adjust strategies, and find new ways to grow. This requires vision and insight—being able to see where the market is heading, what the competition is doing, and how to capitalize on opportunities before others do. But it also requires an understanding of risk, something that every successful King must master.

Risk is a key part of the King's journey. In order to rise to the top, the King must be willing to step out of their comfort zone, to make bold decisions that may not always pay off but could potentially lead to great success. This could mean taking on debt to fund expansion, investing in new technologies, or entering a new market without the guarantee of success. It's about calculated risk—the understanding that sometimes the only way to achieve greatness is by risking what you have for the possibility of something greater.

However, this constant risk-taking isn't just about the King's financial well-being; it's about the well-being of the entire kingdom. The King's decisions can impact the lives of the Royal and the Servants, and with that responsibility comes immense pressure. The King must balance the desire to grow with the need to maintain stability. While the Royal manages the day-to-day operations, the King must keep an eye on the bigger picture, ensuring that the business continues to thrive in the long term.

The King's Vision: Maintaining Focus on the Future

One of the defining qualities of a successful King is their ability to maintain a clear vision for the future. The King's vision is the guiding force behind the entire empire. While others may be focused on immediate tasks or short-term goals, the King must always be looking ahead, thinking about the next step and the next opportunity.

The King's vision is not just about profits; it's about creating something meaningful that lasts. Whether the King is building a company from the ground up, expanding an existing business, or entering new markets, their focus is on long-term success. The King must be able to inspire others with their vision, to communicate their ideas clearly and effectively to the Royal and the Servants, and to convince them that their efforts are part of something greater than themselves.

This vision is what drives the King forward, even in the face of adversity. When the challenges seem insurmountable and the risks too high, the King's vision serves as both a guide and a motivator. It's the North Star that keeps the King on course, even when the winds of uncertainty blow strong. Without a clear vision, the King risks losing direction, and with that loss of direction comes the potential for failure.

The King's Education: Leveraging Knowledge

While financial freedom is certainly a privilege of the King, it is not the sole factor that leads to success. Many Kings rise to power not just because they have financial resources, but because they know how to leverage those resources in ways that others cannot. Education plays a significant role in the King's ability to succeed.

The King's education goes beyond formal schooling or degrees. It is the accumulation of experiences, insights, and knowledge that the King uses to make informed decisions. Education for the King is about understanding markets, reading trends, and knowing how to utilize human resources effectively. It's about understanding the nuances of leadership, negotiation, and risk management. A successful King surrounds themselves with people who complement their knowledge and fill gaps where they may not have expertise, but they themselves must always be learning, growing, and adapting to the ever-changing landscape of business.

The King must understand that knowledge is power. The more they know, the better they can position their kingdom for success. And this knowledge isn't limited to the financial side of things—it's about understanding people, understanding leadership, and understanding how to create an environment where the Royal and the Servants can thrive.

The King's Role: Leadership Beyond the Numbers

Being a King is about more than simply controlling wealth; it is about leadership. The King is the ultimate decision-maker, the final authority on all matters related to the business. But leadership is not just about having the final say; it's about inspiring others, guiding the organization, and motivating the Royal and the Servants to work toward the shared vision.

The King's leadership goes beyond the numbers and financial spreadsheets. It is about setting the tone for the culture of the organization. The King is responsible for creating an environment where the Royal and the Servants feel valued, where their contributions are recognized, and where they are motivated to do their best work. A King who does not understand the importance of culture, who does not foster an environment of trust and mutual respect, will struggle to maintain their empire.

The King must also lead with integrity. Their actions, decisions, and values must reflect the standards they expect from the entire organization. A King who leads with transparency and accountability sets the tone for the entire kingdom. Leadership is not just about making the right decisions; it is about making decisions that are in alignment with the kingdom's values and long-term goals.

The King's Empire: Building and Expanding

The King's empire is not static. It grows, evolves, and adapts to the changing world. Whether through organic growth, acquisitions, or innovations, the King must always be thinking about the next step. The empire must expand, and this expansion requires vision, foresight, and the ability to execute.

A successful King does not rest on their laurels. They understand that building an empire is a continuous process. Every decision they make must be focused on growth—growth of the business, growth of their people, and growth of their vision. The King must always be looking for ways to push the boundaries of what is possible, to redefine the status quo, and to create new opportunities for both themselves and the kingdom.

The King's Legacy

Finally, the King must think about their legacy. The true mark of a King is not just the empire they build, but the lasting impact they leave behind. What will the King's empire stand for? What values will it uphold? How will it be remembered?

The King's legacy is built not just on financial success, but on the impact they have on the lives of the Royal and the Servants. It is about creating an organization that will stand the test of time, that will continue to thrive even after the King has moved on. A legacy is built on the foundation of the King's vision, their leadership, and the empire they create for future generations.

Chapter 3:

The Royal's Crown: Leadership and Stability

The Royal sits between two worlds: the King's grand vision and the Servant's daily grind. Positioned at the helm of an organization, they play a crucial role in making sure that the empire not only survives but thrives. The Royal's role is that of a bridge, the link that connects the high-level strategy of the King with the day-to-day operations of the Servants. The Royal's leadership is the backbone of the kingdom's functionality, as they ensure the wheels of the business turn smoothly and efficiently.

While the King enjoys the financial freedom that comes with ownership, the Royal's position offers stability but not the same level of autonomy. The Royal's success depends on their ability to translate the King's vision into actionable tasks and to manage the resources, people, and systems required to bring those tasks to life. They are responsible for keeping the balance between the ideals of the King and the practical needs of the Servants. The Royal must motivate, guide, and lead the people of the kingdom while ensuring the kingdom's infrastructure and systems are maintained and improved. This chapter will explore the unique challenges faced by the Royal, the qualities that define effective leadership, and the critical role they play in stabilizing and driving the kingdom's success.

The Royal's Role: A Balancing Act

The Royal's position is one of constant balancing. They sit in the middle of the hierarchy, accountable to the King for executing their vision while simultaneously addressing the needs and concerns of the Servants. This is where the tension often lies. On the one hand, the Royal must act as an extension of the King's leadership, ensuring the organization is aligned with the King's strategic goals. On the other hand, they must maintain a keen awareness of the Servants' realities, addressing their challenges and motivations in a way that ensures smooth operations and high morale.

For the Royal, leadership is never a one-size-fits-all approach. They must tailor their management style to different individuals, teams, and circumstances, all while ensuring that the organization moves cohesively toward the overarching goals set by the King. The Royal has the difficult task of being both the enforcer of the King's will and the voice of reason for the Servants. This dual responsibility can create friction, especially when the demands of the King seem unrealistic or when the Servants feel overburdened. The Royal must find a way to bring these two forces together, to motivate both the King and the Servants to work toward a common goal.

In addition to their leadership role, the Royal is also tasked with overseeing the systems that keep the kingdom operational. They are responsible for the organizational infrastructure—everything from the company's financial systems and supply chains to its human resources and technological infrastructure. The Royal ensures that all of these systems are working together seamlessly, with no one part out of sync. This involves problem-solving, innovation, and continuous improvement. While the King may make the big, strategic decisions, it is the Royal who must implement those decisions on the ground.

Financial Stability: The Royal's Dependence on the Organization

While the King enjoys financial freedom, the Royal's wealth and success are tied directly to the organization's prosperity. The Royal has financial stability, but their stability is contingent on the health of the organization. Their role requires constant attention to the bottom line, ensuring that the business remains profitable and that resources are allocated effectively. They do not have the same luxury as the King to take risks without considering the consequences. The Royal must always weigh decisions carefully, ensuring that they maintain a balance between risk and stability.

The Royal's financial security is often linked to their compensation, which can include a salary, bonuses, and potentially even equity in the business. However, unlike the King, who owns the business and controls its financial future, the Royal's income is generally determined by their role within the organization. This means that while the Royal enjoys a level of comfort, they also face a unique set of pressures. They do not have the freedom to make radical changes without considering the impact on their financial stability, as the success of the business directly influences their own earnings.

This financial reality often means that the Royal must make difficult choices that balance both the long-term needs of the business and their own immediate financial considerations. The Royal cannot afford to take unnecessary risks, as the stability they rely on is tied to the success of the business. This is why the Royal's role is often described as the most challenging in the hierarchy: they must maintain stability and balance, ensuring that the kingdom runs smoothly while also supporting the larger vision of the King.

Managing People: The Royal's Leadership and Influence

One of the most critical aspects of the Royal's role is managing people. As the leader of the kingdom, the Royal must ensure that the people who work within it are motivated, engaged, and productive. This involves building relationships, setting expectations, providing feedback, and offering support when needed. The

Royal is the one who must manage the human capital that drives the business forward.

Leadership is not just about giving orders; it is about influencing others to work toward a common goal. The Royal must have the ability to inspire those under their leadership, making the Servants feel valued and engaged in the work they do. They must understand the motivations of the people in their organization and be able to connect the bigger picture of the King's vision with the everyday tasks that the Servants perform. The Royal must also be adept at managing different personalities, skills, and work styles, as they are responsible for maintaining harmony within the team.

Effective leadership requires emotional intelligence—understanding how to motivate and guide people based on their individual needs and strengths. The

Royal must be a good communicator, able to articulate the goals of the business clearly and ensure that each individual understands their role in achieving those goals. But communication goes both ways. The Royal must also listen to the concerns and feedback of the Servants, understanding the challenges they face and finding solutions that balance the needs of the organization with the needs of the people who make it run.

The Royal as the Bridge Between the King and the Servants

The Royal's position can be described as a bridge between the King and the Servants. They are accountable to the King for the success of the business, but they must also serve the interests of the Servants, ensuring that they have the resources, support, and motivation needed to do their jobs. The Royal often finds themselves in the middle of conflicting interests, having to negotiate between the strategic goals of the King and the practical challenges faced by the Servants.

This balancing act requires diplomacy, negotiation skills, and the ability to manage expectations. The Royal must ensure that the King's vision is communicated effectively to the Servants, but they must also make sure that the Servants' concerns are heard and addressed. This is not always an easy task, as the King's vision may be lofty and ambitious, while the Servants may be dealing with the harsh realities of day-to-day work. The Royal must act as the mediator, ensuring that both sides are working together toward a common goal.

The Royal also plays a key role in maintaining the culture of the organization. The King may set the tone for the values of the company, but it is the Royal who ensures that those values are lived out in the day-to-day operations. The Royal's leadership shapes the way people interact, work together, and approach their tasks. If the Royal is effective, they will create a positive, motivating environment where people feel valued and supported. If the Royal is ineffective, however, they risk creating division and disengagement, which can have a lasting impact on the success of the organization.

The Pressures of Leadership: Stress and Burnout

While the Royal's position comes with stability, it also comes with a significant amount of pressure. They are responsible for the success of the business on a day-to-day basis, and this pressure can take a toll. The Royal must make decisions that affect the lives of everyone in the organization. If something goes wrong, the Royal is often the one who must address the problem, manage the fallout, and find solutions.

This constant responsibility can lead to stress and burnout. The Royal must be able to handle the pressure that comes with their role while maintaining focus on the long-term vision of the King. This requires resilience, self-awareness, and the ability to manage stress effectively. The Royal must be able to navigate difficult situations, keep the organization running smoothly during times of crisis, and motivate others even when times are tough.

The Royal's Legacy: Building a Strong Foundation

As much as the Royal is focused on the day-to-day needs of the kingdom, they must also think about their legacy. The Royal's legacy is built on the foundation of the systems, structures, and relationships they create within the organization. A successful Royal leaves behind a well-functioning kingdom, one that is capable of thriving without constant intervention. Their leadership should create a culture of excellence, one that is driven by the same vision the King has but is capable of operating independently when necessary.

A Royal's legacy is not just about the results they achieve in their tenure; it's about how they shape the future of the kingdom. Do they leave behind a strong, motivated team? Do they create systems that allow the business to continue growing and improving? Are they remembered as a leader who made decisions that balanced the needs of the business with the well-being of the people? The Royal's legacy is built on these questions.

Conclusion: The Importance of Stability and Leadership

The Royal's role is not an easy one, but it is an incredibly important one. Positioned between the King and the Servants, the Royal is the glue that holds the organization together. They are responsible for maintaining stability, leading the team, and ensuring that the King's vision is executed effectively. The Royal's leadership influences the culture, the success, and the growth of the organization. It is a role that requires a unique combination of skills—vision, empathy, communication, and decision-making.

Without the Royal, the kingdom would be unstable. Without the Royal's leadership, the King's vision would be impossible to achieve, and the Servants would struggle to perform at their best. The Royal is the key to success in the middle of the hierarchy, ensuring that both the King's aspirations and the Servants' needs are met. In the end, the Royal's role is about balance—finding a way to make the vision of the King a reality while keeping the day-to-day operations running smoothly.

Chapter 4:

The Servant's Path: Struggles of the Working Class

The Servant's role in any organization is fundamental. They are the heartbeat of a business, the ones who perform the daily tasks that keep the operations running. Whether it's working on the factory floor, managing customer relations in an office, or maintaining the retail environment, the Servant is the one whose hands are on the ground, ensuring that everything works seamlessly. Despite their indispensable role, many Servants find themselves caught in a cycle of financial struggle. This chapter will explore the unique challenges the working class faces and delve into the factors that often keep them from achieving financial freedom.

While the King and Royal hold leadership roles and benefit from financial freedom or stability, the Servant is often left behind, working tirelessly without the same level of reward. The Servant plays a crucial part in the success of any organization, but their contributions are often undervalued and undercompensated. Despite being essential to the success of the kingdom, the financial struggles they face are significant, and the road to financial independence often feels out of reach. However, these struggles do not define the Servant's future, and with the right mindset and tools, they can rise from these challenges to find success.

The Financial Struggles of the Servant

The financial challenges that many Servants face are not solely due to laziness or lack of ability. Often, it is the result of external factors—systemic barriers, lack of opportunities, and an inability to break free from the cycle of poverty. While many people in the working class are incredibly hardworking and intelligent, they may find themselves trapped due to circumstances beyond their control. These barriers are deeply ingrained in society and can prevent individuals from achieving the financial success they deserve.

One of the most significant barriers to financial freedom for the Servant is the lack of access to quality education. Without access to the proper tools and resources, many Servants are left with limited career prospects. The education system is not always designed to equip individuals with the skills they need to rise above their circumstances. Even those with the desire to succeed may find that their opportunities are limited by the lack of a degree, specialized training, or access to mentorship. These gaps in education and resources can create a significant divide between the working class and those in leadership roles, such as the King or the Royal.

Another key challenge the Servant faces is the absence of opportunities for upward mobility. Often, individuals in working-class jobs do not have the same access to career advancement as those in higher positions. Many are caught in a cycle of low-wage work, where the promise of a better life feels distant and out of reach. This lack of opportunity to move up within an organization can lead to stagnation, with the Servant working in the same role for years without any substantial change in their financial situation.

Moreover, systemic issues such as income inequality, rising living costs, and a lack of job security compound these difficulties. Many Servants are living paycheck to paycheck, struggling to meet their basic needs. When every penny counts, it becomes nearly impossible to save for the future or invest in education and opportunities for growth. The financial instability they experience makes it harder to take the necessary steps toward financial freedom, and they often find themselves stuck in a vicious cycle of financial insecurity.

The Importance of Education: A Path Out of Poverty

For the Servant to break free from financial struggles, education is often the key. This doesn't necessarily mean traditional schooling, but rather the acquisition of skills and knowledge that will enable them to rise above their current position. Education can take many forms—vocational training, on-the-job learning, mentorship, or even self-study. The Servant who is committed to improving their skills and expanding their knowledge will be better positioned to move up within the organization or transition into a new career that offers better financial opportunities.

The world is constantly changing, and those who adapt and continue to learn have a better chance of rising above their current circumstances. The Servant must be proactive about their education, whether that means taking on new responsibilities at work, seeking out professional development opportunities, or exploring new fields altogether. The more knowledge and skills they acquire, the more valuable they become to the organization and the broader job market.

However, education alone is not enough. It is essential that the Servant is able to apply the knowledge they have gained in a way that directly impacts their career. It's not just about having the skills; it's about knowing how to use them to advance their position. A Servant who continues to learn but fails to use that knowledge to their advantage may remain stagnant, unable to break through the barriers that hold them back.

Mindset: The Servant's Most Powerful Tool

While education is crucial, perhaps the most important factor in overcoming financial struggle is mindset. The way the Servant perceives their situation will directly influence their ability to overcome adversity. A Servant who views their position as temporary—who is determined to learn and grow, to improve their skills and mindset—has a much better chance of achieving success than someone who accepts their current circumstances as permanent.

Mindset is about belief—belief in one's ability to improve, to rise, and to succeed. It is about understanding that financial freedom is not an unattainable dream, but something that can be achieved with hard work, dedication, and the right mindset. Many Servants remain trapped in financial insecurity because they don't believe it's possible to change their situation. But the truth is, a shift in mindset is often the first step toward financial freedom.

The Servant must embrace a growth mindset—one that is open to new opportunities and willing to take risks in order to improve. It's about having the drive to overcome obstacles, to push through challenges, and to learn from failure. The Servant must be willing to ask questions, seek help, and not be afraid to take on new responsibilities or step outside of their comfort zone. A mindset focused on growth and improvement is essential to overcoming the financial struggles that hold many in the working class back.

Additionally, a Servant must focus on the long-term goal, even when the immediate situation feels overwhelming. Financial freedom doesn't happen overnight, and it requires consistent effort over time. By setting clear goals, breaking them down into actionable steps, and staying focused on those goals, the Servant can start to move in the right direction. It's about looking beyond the day-to-day struggles and keeping the end goal in sight.

The Power of Persistence: Overcoming Barriers

The road to financial freedom for the Servant is rarely easy. It is filled with obstacles, setbacks, and challenges. But it is also filled with opportunity. The Servant who is willing to persist in the face of adversity has a much higher chance of breaking free from the cycle of financial insecurity. Persistence is about continuing to push forward, even when the road ahead seems difficult or uncertain. It's about refusing to give up, even when it feels like success is out of reach.

Success is rarely linear. There will be times when the Servant faces setbacks—lost jobs, missed opportunities, financial crises—but these setbacks do not define their future. What matters is how they respond. A Servant who faces adversity with resilience, determination, and a commitment to learning will have a much greater chance of breaking free from their current circumstances. It's about picking oneself back up after failure and continuing to move forward.

The Role of Luck: Timing and Opportunity

While hard work and education are key to overcoming financial struggles, there is no denying that luck plays a role in the success of many individuals. Opportunities often arise by chance—whether it's meeting the right person at the right time, finding an unexpected job opening, or receiving a financial windfall. While the Servant cannot always control these moments of luck, they can position themselves to take advantage of them when they arise.

Luck is often a product of preparation. The Servant who has taken the time to educate themselves, build relationships, and stay focused on their goals will be better prepared to capitalize on opportunities when they appear. It's about being in the right place at the right time and being ready to take action when the moment comes. While luck may not always be predictable, the Servant can increase their chances of experiencing it by remaining dedicated to their personal growth and career advancement.

The Servant's Rise: Overcoming the Odds

The journey from financial struggle to financial freedom is not easy, but it is possible. Many Servants have risen from humble beginnings to become leaders, entrepreneurs, and successful business owners. It is a testament to the power of education, mindset, persistence, and yes, sometimes luck. The Servant who is willing to learn, grow, and challenge their own limitations can break free from the cycle of financial struggle and achieve success.

The key is to never stop striving for improvement. No matter how difficult the journey may seem, the Servant can rise, step by step, toward a brighter future. By focusing on the elements that drive success—education, skill, mindset, and persistence—the Servant can overcome the financial barriers that have held them back and unlock the door to a more prosperous future.

Conclusion: The Servant's Potential

The Servant's path is filled with obstacles, but it is also filled with opportunity. Financial freedom may feel out of reach for many in the working class, but with the right mindset, education, and persistence, it is possible to break free from the cycle of financial struggle. The Servant must focus on their growth, learn new skills, and take advantage of every opportunity that comes their way. Though the journey may be long, the Servant's potential for success is limitless.

Chapter 5:

The Kingdom's Economy: Wealth Distribution and Power

In any successful kingdom, wealth and power must be distributed in a way that ensures the system functions effectively. The roles within the kingdom—the King, the Royal, and the Servant—are interdependent, yet their financial realities differ significantly. The King, at the top of the hierarchy, enjoys financial freedom, the Royal benefits from stability, and the Servant often struggles with poverty. This disparity in wealth and power is a fundamental part of the kingdom's economy, and understanding how wealth flows through the organization is key to understanding the larger dynamics at play.

In this chapter, we will explore how wealth is distributed within the kingdom and the different factors that influence the financial realities of the King, the Royal, and the Servant. We will delve into the economic systems, structures, and opportunities that shape these dynamics, and examine how each role contributes to the creation and flow of wealth. Through this exploration, we will better understand how the kingdom's economy works and the forces that determine the financial outcomes for each member of the kingdom.

Wealth Distribution: The King's Financial Freedom

The King, at the apex of the organization, enjoys financial freedom—the ability to live without the constraints of a paycheck or the constant worry of financial insecurity. This freedom is a direct result of the King's ownership of the organization and the wealth that they have created through their vision, innovation, and leadership. The King's financial reality is tied to the success of the organization, and their wealth is a reflection of the value they have built over time.

The King's financial freedom is not just about having money; it's about having the ability to make decisions without worrying about the immediate financial consequences. The King can invest in new ventures, take risks, and expand their empire, knowing that they have the resources to absorb the costs if things don't go according to plan. Their wealth allows them to control their own destiny and the future of the organization they have created.

However, this financial freedom comes with a great deal of responsibility. The King is accountable for the success or failure of the organization, and their wealth is directly tied to the business's performance. This means that the King's wealth is not guaranteed; it requires constant attention, strategic thinking, and risk management. While the King may enjoy the luxury of financial freedom, they must also deal with the pressures that come with managing large amounts of money and the complexity of running a successful business.

The King's wealth is also tied to the broader market forces that affect the economy. Their financial freedom is not solely based on their individual efforts;

it is the result of the market's response to the business they have built. External factors such as market trends, competition, economic conditions, and government regulations all influence the King's financial reality. In this way, the King's wealth is not entirely in their control—it is shaped by a combination of their decisions and external forces.

The Royal's Stability: Between the King and the Servants

The Royal, positioned between the King and the Servants, occupies a unique financial position in the kingdom. The Royal enjoys a level of financial stability but does not experience the same level of freedom that the King does. Their wealth and success are tied to their role within the organization. While the Royal may be well-compensated for their leadership and management, their financial reality is directly linked to the health of the business. If the business succeeds, the Royal shares in the rewards; if the business falters, the Royal may face consequences in the form of lower compensation, fewer resources, or a loss of influence.

The Royal's financial stability is often a product of the organization's success. They are compensated for their ability to execute the King's vision, manage resources, and keep the business running smoothly. This compensation may come in the form of a salary, bonuses, or even equity in the business, but unlike the King, the Royal does not have the ultimate control over the business's financial outcomes. Their financial security depends on the health of the organization and the decisions made by the King.

While the Royal enjoys stability, they are also exposed to the risks of the business. They may face financial setbacks if the business encounters difficulties, and they must balance the demands of the King with the realities of the workforce. The Royal is responsible for making decisions that support the long-term growth of the organization, but they must also be mindful of the financial constraints that may affect their own role and the financial well-being of the Servants.

The Royal's position is often marked by a constant balancing act. They must manage the expectations of the King, who is focused on the long-term vision and growth of the business, while also addressing the immediate needs of the Servants, who are more concerned with job security, wages, and benefits. The Royal's financial stability allows them to be a key decision-maker within the organization, but they must always be mindful of the interconnectedness of the kingdom's economy.

The Servant's Struggle: Barriers to Financial Security

The Servant, at the bottom of the hierarchy, often faces the greatest financial struggles. Their compensation is typically tied to the hours they work and the tasks they complete, and while they may perform the most essential functions in the organization, their pay often does not reflect the value they bring. Many Servants live paycheck to paycheck, constantly worried about making ends meet, paying bills, and covering basic living expenses.

For the Servant, financial insecurity is a constant reality. The wealth generated by the business is not directly shared with the Servant in a way that leads to financial freedom or stability. Instead, the Servant is often caught in a cycle of poverty, unable to break free due to a lack of resources, opportunities, and access to higher-paying roles. Their financial reality is shaped by a variety of factors, including the wages they earn, the cost of living, and the barriers to advancement within the organization.

Despite the essential role that the Servant plays, they are often overlooked when it comes to wealth distribution. The Servant's wages are typically determined by the market rate for their position, and while they may receive raises or bonuses, these increases are often minimal compared to the wealth generated by the business. As a result, many Servants are stuck in low-paying jobs with little opportunity for upward mobility. Even those who work hard, develop skills, and demonstrate loyalty to the organization may find themselves limited in terms of financial advancement.

The financial struggles of the Servant are also compounded by systemic factors that limit their ability to move up within the organization. Lack of access to education, training, and mentorship can prevent the Servant from acquiring the skills needed to qualify for higher-paying positions. Additionally, many Servants face workplace discrimination or bias that limits their opportunities for advancement. This creates a cycle in which the Servant's financial reality is shaped by factors beyond their control, leaving them stuck in positions with little chance for upward mobility.

How Wealth Flows: The Systems and Structures of the Kingdom's Economy

In order for the kingdom to run effectively, wealth must flow through the entire system in a way that supports each of the three roles. The King, the Royal, and the Servant all contribute to the creation and flow of wealth, but the distribution of that wealth is not always equitable. The King's wealth is largely tied to their ownership and control of the organization, while the Royal's wealth is tied to their ability to manage and execute the King's vision. The Servant, on the other hand, creates wealth through their labor, but often sees little of the financial rewards.

The systems and structures that govern the flow of wealth within the kingdom are crucial to understanding the financial realities of each role. The King sets the strategic direction and creates the conditions that allow wealth to be generated, while the Royal ensures that the organization runs efficiently, allocating resources and managing people in a way that maximizes productivity. The Servant, through their labor, contributes directly to the wealth creation process, performing the essential tasks that allow the organization to thrive.

However, despite their contributions, the Servant is often left out of the wealth distribution process. The structures of many organizations are designed to reward ownership and management, while leaving the working class with minimal financial compensation. This creates a stark divide between the King, the Royal, and the Servant. The Servant may work harder than anyone else in the organization, but their compensation rarely reflects the value they add.

This disparity is often a result of the economic structures that govern wealth distribution in society. Many businesses are structured in a way that allows the King and the Royal to accumulate wealth while the Servants remain trapped in low-wage positions. The Servants' wages are often determined by market forces that do not take into account the value they bring to the organization. This creates a situation where the working class is unable to access the same financial opportunities that those at the top enjoy.

The Role of Opportunity in Wealth Creation

Opportunity plays a key role in determining who has access to wealth and who does not. While the King and the Royal have access to resources, networks, and education that allow them to build and maintain wealth, the Servant often lacks these same opportunities. The financial reality of the Servant is shaped by the opportunities available to them, and without access to education, mentorship, and career advancement, the Servant is often unable to break free from the cycle of poverty.

One of the most important factors in addressing the disparities in wealth distribution is the creation of opportunities for the Servant to rise. Providing access to education, training, and mentorship can help the Servant acquire the skills needed to move up within the organization and achieve financial stability. Similarly, creating pathways for advancement within the organization—where merit, performance, and dedication are rewarded—can help bridge the gap between the King, the Royal, and the Servant.

Conclusion: The Interdependence of Wealth and Power

In the kingdom's economy, wealth and power are distributed in a way that reflects the roles of the King, the Royal, and the Servant. While the King enjoys financial freedom, the Royal experiences stability, and the Servant struggles with poverty, all three roles are essential to the functioning of the organization. Each contributes to the creation and flow of wealth, but the distribution of that wealth is not always equitable. The economic structures and systems in place often favor those at the top, leaving the working class with limited financial security and upward mobility.

In order for the kingdom to run effectively, wealth must flow in a way that supports all three roles. By addressing the barriers to opportunity and creating systems that reward hard work, dedication, and merit, it is possible to create a more equitable distribution of wealth. The King, the Royal, and the Servant all play crucial roles in the success of the organization, and by understanding how wealth is distributed and how each role contributes to the larger system, we can work toward a more balanced and fair economy.

Chapter 6:

The Royal's Dilemma: Balancing Leadership and Compassion

In any organization, the Royal plays a unique and vital role. Positioned between the King, who is the visionary and owner, and the Servants, who are the hardworking backbone of the organization, the Royal is tasked with executing the King's vision while ensuring the day-to-day operations run smoothly. This responsibility is not just logistical but emotional, as the Royal must manage the people within the organization, many of whom may struggle financially and face personal challenges.

The Royal's dilemma stems from the tension between their loyalty to the King, the business's financial goals, and their responsibility to the Servants, who rely on their leadership for stability, fairness, and empathy. While the Royal enjoys financial stability through their leadership role, they are also caught in the often difficult position of balancing the human element of leadership with the financial demands of running a business. This chapter will delve into the complexities of the Royal's role and explore how they navigate the internal struggle of leading with both empathy and efficiency, compassion and results.

The Royal's Position: A Bridge Between Two Worlds

The Royal's position is a delicate one. On the one hand, they are the King's representative in the organization, responsible for translating the King's vision into practical actions that will drive the company forward. The Royal ensures that the big-picture strategy set by the King is executed and that the business remains profitable, competitive, and efficient. On the other hand, the Royal must also manage the people within the organization—individuals with their own needs, desires, and struggles. The Royal is expected to understand the daily challenges faced by the Servants and lead them in a way that makes them feel valued, motivated, and fairly compensated.

This dual role creates an internal conflict for the Royal. They must be loyal to the King, execute the business's objectives, and ensure profitability, but they must also be compassionate toward the Servants, many of whom are underpaid, overworked, and financially insecure. This balancing act requires exceptional leadership skills, emotional intelligence, and the ability to adapt to the needs of both the organization and its employees.

While the Royal enjoys financial stability, their success is still linked to the performance of the organization. They cannot simply act out of kindness or empathy—they must also maintain the financial health of the business. This means that while they may feel compassion for the struggles of the Servants, they must also make tough decisions that could affect the workforce's morale or financial well-being. The Royal's challenge is to balance these two conflicting priorities while remaining a strong, effective leader.

The Royal's Internal Struggle: Financial Stability vs. Compassion

The Royal's financial stability is often directly tied to the success of the business, but unlike the King, the Royal does not have ultimate control over the organization's wealth. The Royal's compensation, though typically generous, is usually based on the organization's profitability and growth. The better the business performs, the better the Royal's compensation, bonuses, and incentives will be. This creates pressure for the Royal to focus on financial outcomes—on increasing efficiency, cutting costs, maximizing profits, and achieving the strategic goals set by the King.

However, the Royal is not immune to the personal challenges that the Servants face. They, too, have likely come from humble beginnings or worked their way up through the ranks, and they may have a deep empathy for the struggles of those who are financially insecure. The Royal may understand that many Servants live paycheck to paycheck, dealing with the stress of financial instability, and may feel conflicted when making decisions that could affect their livelihood.

For example, the Royal may have to decide whether to implement a cost-saving measure that could result in layoffs or reduced hours for certain employees. They may have to manage a budget that requires reducing employee benefits or limiting wage increases, even though they understand that these actions will disproportionately affect the working class. In these moments, the Royal faces a moral dilemma: how can they balance their loyalty to the King's financial goals with their compassion for the Servants who will suffer as a result of those decisions?

Leadership with Empathy: Understanding the Needs of the Servants

Effective leadership is rooted in empathy—the ability to understand and share the feelings of others. The Royal must be able to see the challenges faced by the Servants and respond with compassion and support. They must recognize that the Servants are not just numbers on a spreadsheet—they are individuals with personal struggles, hopes, and dreams. Many of the Servants are likely living in difficult financial circumstances, working multiple jobs, or struggling to provide for their families. The Royal must understand these pressures and find ways to support the Servants without compromising the needs of the organization.

Empathy, however, does not mean compromising the business's goals or ignoring the financial realities that come with running a company. The Royal must be able to balance compassion with efficiency, understanding that while the Servants are the heart of the organization, their needs must be weighed against the business's bottom line. This requires a delicate approach—one where the Royal listens to the Servants' concerns, communicates transparently, and takes action where possible, without sacrificing the profitability and long-term goals of the business.

An empathetic Royal knows how to motivate their team, even in difficult times. They recognize that the Servants' engagement and morale are key to the success of the business. If the Servants feel undervalued, overworked, or unappreciated, their productivity and commitment to the company will suffer. The Royal's ability to communicate effectively, recognize hard work, and provide emotional support can help maintain a positive work environment and foster loyalty among the workforce.

Managing Expectations: The Royal's Role as Mediator

The Royal must also act as a mediator between the King's high-level vision and the practical realities faced by the Servants. The King's goals for the organization are often focused on growth, expansion, and profitability, but these goals can sometimes feel disconnected from the day-to-day realities of the workforce. The Servants, on the other hand, are more concerned with job security, fair compensation, and a stable work environment.

The Royal's role is to bridge this gap, ensuring that the King's vision is communicated clearly to the

Servants while also making sure that the needs of the workforce are considered in the decision-making process. This requires both communication skills and emotional intelligence. The Royal must be able to manage the expectations of both the King and the Servants, making sure that both sides understand each other's perspectives and that decisions are made in a way that is fair and effective.

For example, if the King sets a goal to increase profits by reducing costs, the Royal must figure out how to implement this strategy without alienating the Servants or compromising their job security. They may need to find creative solutions, such as improving operational efficiency, implementing training programs that increase productivity, or offering incentives for employees who meet specific targets. The Royal's ability to find compromises that address both the business's goals and the Servants' needs is a key aspect of their leadership.

The Royal's Responsibility: Decision-Making in Difficult Times

The Royal's responsibility is especially crucial in difficult times—during financial downturns, market disruptions, or moments of crisis. When the organization faces challenges that threaten its financial health, the Royal must make tough decisions. These decisions may involve reducing staff, cutting wages, or scaling back employee benefits. The Royal must carry the weight of these decisions, knowing that their actions will directly impact the Servants' financial well-being and security.

In these moments, the Royal must lead with transparency and empathy. They must communicate openly with the Servants, explaining the reasons behind the decisions and offering as much support as possible. While the Royal cannot avoid making difficult choices, they can mitigate the impact of these choices by providing resources, training, or assistance that helps the Servants navigate through the challenges.

For example, if layoffs are necessary, the Royal must ensure that those affected are treated with dignity and respect. They may offer severance packages, outplacement services, or retraining programs to help employees transition to new roles. The Royal's ability to handle these situations with compassion, while also making the necessary financial decisions, will have a lasting impact on the Servants' trust in their leadership.

The Balance of Compassion and Results: Leadership at Its Core

At the heart of the Royal's dilemma is the constant balancing act between compassion and results. The Royal must care deeply about the people they lead, understanding their challenges and striving to provide support. But they must also be results-oriented, focused on achieving the business's goals and ensuring its success. The Royal's ability to navigate this balance is what separates effective leaders from those who struggle to lead successfully.

The Royal must recognize that both compassion and results are necessary for long-term success. Compassion without results leads to an unsustainable business, while results without compassion can lead to a disengaged and unmotivated workforce. The key is to find a way to integrate both into a cohesive leadership style that supports the organization's goals while fostering a positive and supportive work environment.

The Royal's Legacy: Leading with Integrity

The Royal's legacy is defined by their ability to lead with integrity—balancing the financial needs of the organization with the well-being of the people who make it run. By leading with empathy, understanding, and a clear focus on both the business and its workforce, the Royal can create a legacy of strong leadership that is remembered for both its results and its compassion.

In the end, the Royal's challenge is to ensure that the kingdom's prosperity is built on a foundation of trust, respect, and fairness. The Royal must show that it is possible to lead with both a strong hand and a compassionate heart, and that by doing so, the entire organization can thrive.

Conclusion: A Leader Who Bridges the Gap

The Royal's dilemma is one of the most challenging aspects of leadership within an organization. They must navigate the delicate balance between loyalty to the King's vision and compassion for the Servants. This balance requires emotional intelligence, strategic thinking, and the ability to make tough decisions that benefit the long-term success of the organization while also considering the human element of leadership. The Royal's success is built not only on their ability to execute the King's vision but on their capacity to lead with empathy, transparency, and integrity, ensuring that both the business and its people thrive.

Chapter 7:

The Servant's Drive: Overcoming Financial Struggles

The Servant, positioned at the base of the organizational hierarchy, is often the most financially vulnerable of the three roles—the King, the Royal, and the Servant. Yet, despite the heavy financial burdens they face, the Servant is not without potential. The path from financial insecurity to financial freedom may be long and arduous, but it is not impossible. Through drive, dedication, and strategic planning, the Servant can break free from the cycle of financial struggle and work their way up the ranks of the organization.

In this chapter, we will explore how the Servant can overcome their financial struggles by taking a proactive approach to their financial situation. It's not enough to simply work hard or rely on raw intelligence —success requires a deeper, more strategic effort. The Servant must be intentional about their growth and development, using the resources available to them to climb the ladder of success. By focusing on self-improvement, networking, and skill development, the Servant can pave the way toward greater financial security, and eventually, to positions of greater power, such as the Royal or even the King.

The Servant's Financial Reality: Understanding the Struggles

For many, the financial struggle of the Servant is a daily reality. Wages are often low, and the cost of living continues to rise, making it difficult to break free from a paycheck-to-paycheck existence. The Servant's financial vulnerability is exacerbated by a lack of access to wealth-building opportunities, limited education, and few resources for personal and professional development. Despite working hard, the Servant is often stuck in a cycle of financial insecurity, with little chance of upward mobility.

In many cases, the Servant's position within the organization reflects broader systemic issues. The working class often faces structural barriers that limit their ability to improve their financial situation. These barriers may include a lack of access to higher-paying job opportunities, limited educational resources, and insufficient support for professional development. The Servant may work tirelessly, but without the right tools, guidance, and opportunities, their financial situation remains stagnant.

While these struggles are significant, it's important to recognize that they are not insurmountable. The Servant's financial vulnerability may be a result of external factors, but their response to these challenges is within their control. The key to overcoming these struggles lies in developing a proactive, strategic approach to financial success. By focusing on self-improvement, building key skills, and seizing opportunities, the Servant can break the cycle of financial hardship and start on a path toward greater financial security and professional growth.

The Power of Education: Unlocking Opportunities for Advancement

Education is one of the most powerful tools the Servant has to overcome financial struggles. While formal education—such as earning a degree—can provide access to higher-paying jobs, it is not the only form of education that matters. Education, in this context, is about acquiring knowledge, skills, and experiences that enhance the Servant's value in the workplace and increase their potential for advancement.

Many Servants feel that education is out of their reach due to financial constraints or a lack of access to higher learning institutions. However, there are many ways to invest in education without incurring significant debt or sacrificing financial security. Online courses, workshops, certifications, and vocational training programs can provide the skills necessary to move up within the organization or transition into a new field. These educational opportunities are often more affordable, flexible, and accessible than traditional college or university programs.

In addition to formal education, the Servant should seek to learn as much as possible on the job. Learning from colleagues, supervisors, and mentors is an invaluable form of education that can help the Servant build key skills and knowledge necessary for upward mobility. By seeking out new challenges and responsibilities within their current role, the Servant can gain hands-on experience that will make them more competitive for promotions or new job opportunities.

The Servant should also focus on developing a mindset of continuous learning. The business world is always evolving, and the Servant must remain adaptable to stay relevant in their field. By embracing a growth mindset and continually seeking opportunities to expand their knowledge and skills, the Servant can increase their value and improve their chances of advancement. Education is not just about formal schooling—it's about a lifelong commitment to personal and professional growth.

Self-Improvement: The Key to Personal and Financial Growth

Beyond education, self-improvement is a critical element in overcoming financial struggles. The Servant must take ownership of their personal development and work to improve their habits, mindset, and work ethic. Financial success is often a result of hard work, persistence, and the ability to overcome challenges. By focusing on self-improvement, the Servant can increase their chances of success both in their current role and in future opportunities.

One of the most important aspects of self-improvement is developing discipline and consistency. The Servant must be willing to put in the effort and stay committed to their goals, even when things get tough. Building good habits—such as setting aside time each day for personal development, working efficiently, and maintaining a positive attitude—will have a lasting impact on the Servant's ability to move forward. The Servant should set clear goals for both their personal and professional growth and take actionable steps each day to achieve them.

Additionally, the Servant should focus on building resilience and emotional intelligence. Financial struggles can take a toll on one's mental health, and the ability to cope with stress, setbacks, and uncertainty is essential for long-term success. By developing emotional intelligence—such as self-awareness, empathy, and emotional regulation—the Servant can better navigate the ups and downs of their journey, maintain their motivation, and remain focused on their goals.

Self-improvement also involves building confidence. The Servant must believe in their own potential and recognize that they have the ability to overcome challenges and rise to higher levels of success. Confidence is key to taking on new opportunities, seeking promotions, and pushing through obstacles. By nurturing a strong sense of self-belief, the Servant can move past self-doubt and pursue their financial and professional goals with greater determination.

Networking: Building Connections for Career Advancement

Networking is another powerful tool that the Servant can use to overcome financial struggles. Many people are able to advance in their careers not solely because of their hard work or education, but because they have access to opportunities through their connections. Networking can help the Servant expand their professional circle, gain access to valuable mentorship, and open doors to job opportunities that might otherwise be out of reach.

Building relationships with colleagues, supervisors, and industry professionals can provide the Servant with the guidance, advice, and support they need to advance in their career. The Servant should attend industry events, conferences, and networking groups to meet people who can offer insight into the field and potential career opportunities. Mentorship is also a key part of networking. By seeking out mentors—whether inside or outside of the organization—the Servant can gain wisdom from those who have already navigated the challenges of career advancement.

Networking also provides the Servant with access to valuable information. The Servant can learn about job openings, industry trends, and the skills that are in demand, all of which can help them make informed decisions about their career. By connecting with others, the Servant can better position themselves for success and increase their chances of moving up the ladder.

Developing a Mindset for Upward Mobility

One of the most important factors in the Servant's ability to overcome financial struggles is their mindset. The Servant must believe that they have the potential to rise, that they can break free from their current circumstances and achieve greater financial success. This mindset is the foundation for all other efforts—education, self-improvement, networking, and skill development. Without the belief in their own potential, the Servant may struggle to find the motivation to take the necessary steps toward financial improvement.

The Servant must adopt a growth mindset—an attitude that embraces learning, resilience, and the belief that success comes through effort and persistence. With a growth mindset, the Servant will view challenges as opportunities to learn and grow, rather than as insurmountable obstacles. They will be more likely to seek out new opportunities, take on new responsibilities, and invest in their own development.

Additionally, the Servant should cultivate a mindset of abundance. Many people from lower-income backgrounds operate with a scarcity mindset, believing that there are limited opportunities available to them. However, by adopting a mindset of abundance, the Servant can open themselves up to the possibility of growth and success. They must believe that there are ample opportunities for everyone, and that they have the ability to seize those opportunities when they arise.

Strategic Planning: Mapping the Path to Success

Finally, the Servant must develop a clear plan for their financial and professional future. While hard work and determination are essential, the Servant must also take a strategic approach to their success. This involves setting long-term goals, identifying the steps required to achieve those goals, and breaking those steps down into manageable tasks.

Strategic planning involves assessing where the Servant currently stands, where they want to go, and how they can get there. This may involve setting specific career goals, such as moving into a managerial position or transitioning to a higher-paying role in a different industry. The Servant must identify the skills, experiences, and resources needed to achieve these goals, and develop a plan to acquire them.

By creating a roadmap for success and taking consistent, focused action, the Servant can overcome financial struggles and move closer to their financial and professional goals.

Conclusion: The Servant's Path to Financial Freedom

The path to overcoming financial struggles is not an easy one, but it is possible. The Servant has the potential to rise from financial insecurity to financial freedom, but this requires more than just hard work. It requires a proactive, strategic approach that includes education, self-improvement, networking, and the development of key skills. By cultivating a growth mindset, building resilience, and planning strategically for the future, the Servant can break free from the cycle of poverty and achieve greater financial security.

The journey will not be quick or easy, but it is one that is achievable through dedication, perseverance, and a commitment to personal and professional growth. Through their drive and determination, the Servant can rise to new heights, creating a future where financial struggles are no longer a burden, and where they can enjoy the same opportunities for success as the King and the Royal.

Chapter 8:

The King's Legacy: Creating a Sustainable Kingdom

A true King's legacy is not built on the wealth they accumulate during their reign; it is about creating a kingdom that will endure long after they have stepped down from the throne. The King's success is not simply defined by personal wealth or power; it is measured by the sustainability of the organization they've built, by how well the kingdom supports not only their own financial freedom but also the growth and stability of the Royal and the Servants. The strength of the kingdom is reflected in the success of all those who live within it, and a truly great King will invest in their people to ensure that the kingdom thrives for generations.

A sustainable kingdom is one where financial freedom, stability, and growth are shared by everyone—the King, the Royal, and the Servants. It is an organization that values the contribution of each individual, recognizing that the success of the whole is built on the success of each part. This chapter will explore how the King can create such a kingdom, where the wealth they generate flows through the entire system, creating opportunities for all roles and ensuring the long-term prosperity of the organization. The King must also recognize that their legacy is not just about leaving behind a vast fortune; it is about building a foundation that allows the kingdom to thrive long after their time at the helm.

The King's Vision: Building for the Long-Term

A great King begins with a vision—a clear, compelling idea of what the kingdom should be and what it can become. The King's vision is not limited to the immediate needs of the business or the personal gains they can achieve. Instead, it encompasses the long-term growth of the organization, ensuring that it will remain viable and prosperous for future generations.

This vision must be far-reaching, looking beyond the present moment to understand the challenges and opportunities that lie ahead. The King must think strategically about the future, anticipating changes in the market, technology, and global trends. A sustainable kingdom is one that is prepared for these shifts and is capable of adapting to them. The King's vision must include a clear roadmap for growth, a commitment to sustainability, and an understanding that the organization's success is not solely dependent on short-term profits but on long-term strategies that benefit everyone involved.

The King's vision should also recognize that the organization's success is intertwined with the success of the people who make it run. Financial freedom, stability, and opportunity must be shared, ensuring that the Royal and the Servants are not left behind as the business grows. This requires a commitment to investing in people—offering them the tools, education, and resources they need to succeed.

Investing in People: The Foundation of a Sustainable Kingdom

One of the most important ways a King can create a sustainable kingdom is by investing in their people. The Royal and the Servants are the lifeblood of the organization, and their success is critical to the long-term health of the business. A King who recognizes this will understand that their own success is dependent on the growth and development of those around them.

Investing in people begins with offering them the tools they need to grow professionally. This includes providing opportunities for education, training, and mentorship. By investing in the development of the Royal and the Servants, the King creates an environment where talent is nurtured, and individuals have the chance to rise within the organization.

For the Royal, this may mean providing leadership training, encouraging innovation, and fostering an environment where they can learn to manage teams effectively and execute the King's vision. For the Servants, it may involve offering opportunities for upskilling or providing access to resources that allow them to improve their qualifications and position within the organization. Investing in people ensures that the kingdom has the human capital necessary to thrive and adapt in an ever-changing business landscape.

Moreover, investing in people also means creating a culture that values collaboration, respect, and fairness. A sustainable kingdom cannot be built on exploitation or division. The King must foster a culture where every role is valued and every contribution is recognized. When people feel supported and valued, they are more likely to remain committed to the success of the organization, which in turn creates a stable and thriving kingdom.

Creating Opportunities for Growth: Elevating the Royal and the Servants

For a kingdom to be truly sustainable, it is essential that all roles—whether the King, the Royal, or the Servants—have opportunities for growth and advancement. The King must actively create pathways that allow individuals to rise within the organization, whether through promotions, lateral moves, or the development of new roles that meet the evolving needs of the business.

A key part of this is ensuring that the Royal is empowered to manage the people within the organization, creating systems that encourage performance and reward success. This may include clear paths for advancement, professional development opportunities, and regular performance reviews that identify areas for improvement and growth. The Royal's role is crucial in ensuring that the Servants have access to these opportunities and that there is transparency in how individuals can advance within the kingdom.

For the Servants, a sustainable kingdom means offering them a chance to improve their financial situation and rise through the ranks. It means providing a clear, achievable path to promotion, where hard work and dedication are rewarded with higher compensation, more responsibility, and opportunities to take on leadership roles. This can be done through training programs, mentoring, and providing the resources necessary for the Servants to gain the skills and knowledge needed for upward mobility. By creating opportunities for growth within the organization, the King helps ensure that the Servants are not stuck in positions of financial insecurity but are instead empowered to build better lives for themselves and their families.

Ensuring Financial Stability: A Shared Responsibility

A sustainable kingdom is one where financial stability is shared among all roles. While the King may enjoy financial freedom and the Royal may experience financial stability, the Servants should also have the opportunity to achieve financial security. The King's legacy must include a kingdom where wealth is distributed in a way that allows everyone to thrive, and where the success of the business benefits not only the top levels of leadership but also those who perform the essential work that keeps the business running.

To ensure financial stability across the kingdom, the King must create compensation structures that are fair and equitable. This includes providing competitive wages for the Servants, offering benefits that support their well-being, and creating opportunities for bonuses, raises, and profit-sharing. The Royal should play an active role in ensuring that compensation reflects both the market and the contributions of the employees.

A sustainable kingdom is one where the financial success of the organization benefits everyone, not just the King and the Royal. By offering competitive compensation and opportunities for financial growth, the King can create a stable and committed workforce, ensuring that the kingdom remains prosperous over the long term.

Building a Legacy: A Kingdom That Lasts

A true King's legacy is not just about the wealth they accumulate during their reign but about building something that endures. It is about creating a kingdom that continues to thrive long after they have moved on, where the Royal and the Servants are able to succeed and carry the organization forward. The King's legacy is built on the foundation of their leadership, the values they instill in their people, and the systems they put in place to ensure the kingdom's sustainability.

The King must also recognize that their legacy is about creating opportunities for the next generation of leaders. This means investing in leadership development, ensuring that the Royal and the Servants have access to the skills, experiences, and mentorship needed to take on greater responsibilities and continue the kingdom's success. The King's legacy is also about creating a culture of innovation, where new ideas are encouraged, and where the kingdom is always looking for ways to improve and adapt.

One of the most powerful ways a King can create a lasting legacy is by fostering a sense of pride, loyalty, and commitment within the kingdom. When people believe in the mission of the organization and feel valued, they are more likely to dedicate themselves to its long-term success. The King's legacy is not just built on profits or growth but on the impact they have had on the lives of the people they lead.

The Role of Sustainability in Creating a Kingdom of Lasting Value

The sustainability of the kingdom depends on its ability to evolve and adapt to changing conditions. The King's vision must be flexible, able to respond to market shifts, technological advancements, and changes in the workforce. A sustainable kingdom is one that continually seeks improvement, invests in innovation, and remains ahead of the curve.

Environmental sustainability is another critical aspect of creating a kingdom that thrives for generations. The King must consider the long-term impact of their decisions on the environment and ensure that the kingdom's practices support a healthy planet for future generations. This can involve adopting sustainable business practices, reducing waste, and promoting environmental responsibility within the organization.

Sustainability also includes social responsibility. A truly sustainable kingdom supports the well-being of its community and society as a whole. The King should be committed to ethical business practices, fair treatment of employees, and contributing positively to the communities in which the organization operates. By fostering a culture of social responsibility, the King creates a kingdom that is not only financially successful but also a force for good in the world.

Conclusion: The King's Legacy: A Kingdom That Thrives

A true King's legacy is defined not by the wealth they accumulate but by the kingdom they build—a kingdom that supports the Royal and the Servants and creates opportunities for everyone to thrive. The King's legacy is one of sustainability, where financial freedom, stability, and growth are shared across all roles. By investing in their people, creating opportunities for growth, and ensuring that the kingdom remains adaptable and responsible, the King can build an organization that endures long after their reign.

Ultimately, the King's legacy is not about leaving behind a fortune but about building a kingdom that continues to thrive and grow, where all roles—whether the King, the Royal, or the Servant—can succeed together. This is the true mark of a great King: the ability to create a sustainable, thriving kingdom that endures for generations.

Chapter 9:

Unity in the Kingdom: A Balanced Economy

For a kingdom to function effectively, the roles of King, Royal, and Servant must work together in harmony. While each role is distinct, their interdependence is crucial to creating a thriving, balanced economy. The success of the kingdom depends not just on the leadership and vision of the King, nor the management and execution of the Royal, but also on the essential labor and contributions of the Servants. When all three roles are aligned, the kingdom thrives.

However, when these roles are disconnected, the entire structure can falter.

This chapter explores how unity within the kingdom is the key to maintaining a balanced economy. It will focus on how collaboration, communication, and mutual respect between the King, the Royal, and the Servants can foster an environment where everyone can succeed. By recognizing their interdependence and supporting one another in their individual and collective journeys, the kingdom can become a place of growth, prosperity, and sustainability for all.

The Interdependence of the King, Royal, and Servant

The King, Royal, and Servant are each critical to the success of the kingdom, but their contributions differ.

The King brings vision, ownership, and financial freedom to the organization. The Royal manages the daily operations and ensures that the vision is translated into action. The Servants perform the essential tasks that keep the kingdom running and enable its growth.

While their roles differ, the success of the kingdom is not possible without the active participation of each. The King's wealth and vision cannot be realized without the Royal's ability to manage the business effectively, and the Royal's leadership would be undermined without the support of the Servants. Similarly, the Servants' work would be meaningless without the direction provided by the King and the Royal. This interdependence forms the backbone of a balanced economy, where each role contributes to the greater success of the whole.

It is essential for each role to understand its place in the broader system and to recognize the importance of the others. The King must understand that their wealth and freedom are built on the labor of the Servants and the execution of the Royal. The Royal must understand that their ability to lead depends on the support and hard work of the Servants. And the Servants must understand that they are not merely cogs in the machine, but integral contributors to the organization's success, whose efforts are essential to the growth of the kingdom.

When each role recognizes its interdependence and works together in a spirit of collaboration and respect, the kingdom can flourish. However, when these roles become disconnected or one group feels undervalued, the economy of the kingdom suffers, leading to discontent, inefficiency, and stagnation.

The Importance of Collaboration in a Balanced Economy

Collaboration is at the heart of any successful organization. In a kingdom, the King, Royal, and Servant must collaborate at every level to ensure that the vision of the King is brought to life, the operations are managed effectively, and the work is done with dedication and efficiency.

Collaboration between the King and the Royal is necessary for the execution of the King's vision. The King's leadership provides the direction, but it is the Royal's job to ensure that the vision is feasible and actionable. The Royal must provide feedback and offer realistic input to help shape the long-term goals of the kingdom. While the King has the ultimate authority, the Royal's perspective is invaluable in ensuring that the vision aligns with the practical needs of the organization.

Moreover, the Royal and the Servants must also work together in collaboration. The Royal cannot manage the kingdom effectively without understanding the challenges and needs of the Servants. The Servants, in turn, cannot succeed without the guidance, structure, and support provided by the Royal. The Royal must lead with empathy, offering opportunities for growth, recognition, and support while also holding the Servants accountable for their work. At the same time, the Servants must understand that their success is not just about individual achievement but about contributing to the collective success of the organization.

When collaboration is prioritized, both the Royal and the Servants are empowered to perform their roles to the best of their ability. The Royal can provide the support and direction the Servants need, while the Servants can contribute their efforts to achieving the kingdom's goals. Collaboration fosters an environment of mutual respect, where each person's contributions are recognized, and the kingdom can achieve its objectives.

Communication: The Key to Understanding and Success

Communication is the bedrock upon which collaboration is built. In any organization, the flow of information is crucial for ensuring that everyone is aligned and working toward the same goals. For a kingdom to function effectively, communication between the King, Royal, and Servants must be clear, transparent, and frequent.

The King must communicate their vision clearly to the Royal and the Servants, ensuring that everyone understands the long-term goals of the organization and the role they play in achieving them. The Royal must then communicate the King's vision to the Servants in a way that is relatable and actionable. The Servants must understand not only what they are expected to do but why their work is important to the larger success of the kingdom.

Equally important is feedback. The Royal must be receptive to feedback from the Servants, understanding their needs, challenges, and suggestions for improvement. The Royal should create an open and supportive environment where the Servants feel comfortable expressing their concerns and ideas. Likewise, the Servants must be open to feedback from the Royal, understanding that constructive criticism is intended to help them grow and improve.

The King must also communicate with the Royal and Servants regularly to ensure that the business is progressing as planned. They must be open to discussing challenges and adjusting strategies if necessary. A kingdom that thrives on strong communication is one where problems are addressed quickly, successes are celebrated, and everyone feels valued and heard.

Mutual Respect: Fostering a Positive Work Environment

Mutual respect is a fundamental element of any balanced economy. For the kingdom to thrive, the King, Royal, and Servants must all treat each other with dignity and respect. This respect is not simply a matter of politeness; it is about recognizing the intrinsic value of each individual's contribution to the organization.

The King must recognize that their success is intertwined with the success of the Royal and the Servants. The King cannot build their empire without the hard work and dedication of those below them. The Royal must recognize the importance of the Servants' work and treat them as valuable partners in the organization. The Servants must recognize the role that both the King and the Royal play in their success and contribute to the organization's goals with respect and professionalism.

When mutual respect is present in the kingdom, people are more likely to be motivated and engaged. When the Royal listens to the Servants' concerns and treats them with respect, the Servants are more likely to feel valued and perform their work with dedication. Likewise, when the King recognizes the contributions of the Royal and Servants and expresses appreciation, the entire organization is inspired to work harder and smarter.

Mutual respect also means fairness and equity. In a balanced economy, each role is compensated fairly for their contribution to the organization's success. The King, Royal, and Servants all benefit from the growth and prosperity of the kingdom, and their compensation reflects the value they provide. Fairness in compensation and recognition is crucial for maintaining morale and ensuring that all roles are respected.

How Each Role Contributes to the Success of the Kingdom

Each role in the kingdom—whether the King, Royal, or Servant—contributes to the organization's success in unique and essential ways.

The King's contribution is visionary. They set the direction for the kingdom, create the structure that allows the organization to thrive, and provide the resources and leadership necessary to bring the vision to life. The King's role is to ensure that the kingdom grows and adapts to meet the challenges of the future. They must also ensure that the economic structure of the kingdom supports the well-being of all involved, recognizing that their success is tied to the success of those they lead.

The Royal's contribution is managerial. They are responsible for executing the King's vision, managing the day-to-day operations, and ensuring that the organization runs smoothly. The Royal is the one who translates the King's grand plans into actionable steps, managing resources, people, and processes to achieve the kingdom's goals. The Royal's leadership ensures that the business is efficient, productive, and profitable.

The Servants' contribution is foundational. They are the ones who do the essential work that keeps the kingdom running. From manufacturing products to providing customer service, the Servants perform the tasks that are crucial to the kingdom's success. Without their hard work and dedication, the kingdom would not thrive. While they may not hold the same level of power or financial freedom as the King or Royal, their contributions are indispensable to the kingdom's prosperity.

When each role recognizes and appreciates the contributions of the others, the kingdom becomes stronger and more cohesive. Each part of the organization is working toward the same goals, supporting each other in their individual efforts, and contributing to the success of the whole.

The Power of Unity: A Thriving, Balanced Economy

A kingdom is strongest when the King, Royal, and Servants work together in unity. The balance between these roles ensures that the kingdom functions efficiently, that everyone has the opportunity to thrive, and that the organization continues to grow and prosper over time. When the King, Royal, and Servants understand their interdependence and collaborate in the spirit of mutual respect, they create a thriving, balanced economy that benefits everyone involved.

This unity is built on collaboration, communication, and respect. It requires each role to recognize the value of the others and to support one another in the pursuit of the kingdom's goals. It means ensuring that opportunities for growth and success are available to all, and that no one is left behind. A kingdom that is united in purpose and action is a kingdom that will endure, grow, and continue to thrive for generations.

In the end, the success of the kingdom depends not on the individual power of the King or the Royal, but on the collective effort of all three roles working together. When unity is achieved, the economy of the kingdom becomes balanced, sustainable, and prosperous for all.

Chapter 10:

The Kingdom's Future: Building a Legacy for Generations

As we look to the future, the question arises: How can the kingdom evolve? In an ever-changing world, how can the roles of King, Royal, and Servant adapt to modern challenges and opportunities? The business environment, much like society at large, is not static. New technologies, shifting economic forces, cultural changes, and social movements continue to shape the landscape in which organizations operate. A successful kingdom must evolve in response to these changes, ensuring that all roles—whether the King, the Royal, or the Servant—remain relevant and empowered in the future. This chapter explores how the kingdom can adapt to these challenges, create more opportunities for upward mobility, and build a legacy that benefits generations to come.

At its core, the evolution of the kingdom lies in the ability to balance tradition with innovation. While the foundational roles of King, Royal, and Servant will always be crucial to the functioning of the organization, the way these roles are structured and the way the kingdom operates must evolve. This chapter will explore how the roles within the kingdom can shift and grow to meet new demands while still fostering unity and support for all those within the organization.

Adapting to Changing Times: The Evolution of the King's Role

The role of the King is traditionally associated with ownership, vision, and financial freedom. The King is the decision-maker, the one who takes risks to ensure the success and growth of the kingdom. However, as the world changes, so too must the role of the King. Today's King must be both a visionary and a dynamic leader who can adapt to the rapid changes in the business landscape.

Modern challenges, such as technological advancements, global competition, economic instability, and a rapidly shifting workforce, demand a new kind of leadership. The King must be able to recognize emerging trends and harness the potential of innovation to propel the kingdom forward. This requires staying ahead of the curve—not just in terms of market opportunities but also in terms of social responsibility and sustainability. Today's King must understand that true success is not only about financial growth but also about creating an organization that is responsible, ethical, and adaptable in the face of change.

One of the most significant changes to the role of the King is the shift toward a more inclusive and participatory leadership style. In the past, Kings were often solitary decision-makers, wielding power from the top down. Today's King must embrace collaboration and inclusivity. The King's decisions will still guide the kingdom, but the process should involve the Royal and Servants in meaningful ways. By fostering a culture of open communication and shared vision, the King ensures that the entire kingdom is aligned, invested, and empowered to contribute to the organization's success.

Furthermore, as the world becomes increasingly interconnected, the King's role must also include a focus on global stewardship. The King must be aware of their organization's impact on the broader world—environmentally, socially, and economically. Sustainable practices, ethical decision-making, and corporate responsibility are now non-negotiable components of a successful kingdom. The King must also be proactive in embracing diversity, equity, and inclusion, ensuring that their kingdom represents the global society they serve.

The Royal's Evolution: From Manager to Mentor and Leader of Change

As the kingdom evolves, so too must the role of the Royal. Traditionally, the Royal was seen as the manager, the one responsible for executing the King's vision and maintaining the efficiency of the organization. In today's dynamic business world, the Royal's role is expanding beyond management to include mentorship, innovation, and leadership in change.

The modern Royal must understand that leadership is not just about overseeing daily operations—it is about empowering others to reach their full potential. In the future, the Royal's role will involve fostering leadership at every level of the organization. By mentoring and developing future leaders within the organization, the Royal ensures that the kingdom's legacy endures beyond their own tenure. This requires investing in the professional growth of the Servants, encouraging upward mobility, and creating pathways for people to move from entry-level positions to leadership roles.

Additionally, the Royal must take on the role of a change agent within the organization. Today's business environment is marked by constant change—new technologies, evolving consumer preferences, and shifting global dynamics. The Royal must not only manage operations efficiently but also drive the adoption of new ideas and technologies that keep the kingdom competitive. The Royal must lead the charge in creating a culture of innovation, encouraging the exploration of new ideas, products, and services that can position the kingdom for long-term success.

The Royal must also be attuned to the evolving needs of the Servants. As the workforce becomes more diverse and the demands for work-life balance, mental health support, and career advancement increase, the Royal must ensure that the kingdom adapts to these needs. This means creating a work environment that prioritizes flexibility, mental well-being, and opportunities for personal and professional development. By understanding the challenges faced by the Servants and addressing them proactively, the Royal creates an environment of loyalty, trust, and high morale.

The Servant's Evolution: From Worker to Entrepreneur and Stakeholder

The Servant's role is perhaps the most drastically evolving. Traditionally, the Servant was seen as the worker—the person who executes the tasks that keep the organization running. In many ways, the Servant was a cog in the machine. However, as the workforce evolves, so does the role of the Servant. Today, the Servant is being empowered to take on more responsibility, contribute more meaningfully to decision-making, and even become entrepreneurial in their approach to work.

One of the most significant changes for the Servant in the future is the shift from being merely a worker to becoming a stakeholder in the success of the organization. The future of work is moving towards more flexible, decentralized models where employees are not just employees but also active participants in the organization's growth. The Servant can be seen as a partner in the kingdom, someone who shares in both the risks and rewards of the organization. This shift can manifest in profit-sharing programs, equity stakes, or opportunities to contribute to decision-making and innovation.

The Servant must also embrace the evolving nature of work itself. As industries change, the traditional, one-dimensional job roles that defined the past are becoming less relevant. Future Servants will need to be more adaptable, continuously learning new skills and taking on new responsibilities. The future workforce will be marked by its ability to shift roles, work across departments, and become part of collaborative teams that innovate and drive change.

The Servant's path to upward mobility is also evolving. In the past, moving up in the organization was often a slow and rigid process, based on seniority or fixed hierarchical structures. In the future, the Servant's path to success will be more dynamic and based on performance, innovation, and the ability to contribute to the kingdom's long-term goals. The Servant will need to develop entrepreneurial skills, taking initiative and responsibility for their own professional growth. This shift will require the Servant to develop a mindset of continuous learning, innovation, and resilience.

Creating More Opportunities for Upward Mobility

One of the most significant challenges the kingdom faces in the future is how to create more opportunities for upward mobility. In traditional organizational structures, upward mobility was often limited by rigid hierarchies and a lack of access to professional development. The future of the kingdom must be one where individuals, regardless of their starting point, have the opportunity to rise within the organization.

This requires a shift in organizational culture—from one that prioritizes seniority or rigid roles to one that values performance, growth, and potential. The King, Royal, and Servants must work together to create opportunities for mentorship, skill development, and cross-functional collaboration. This will ensure that the workforce is adaptable and can respond to the evolving needs of the business.

The Servants must be given the tools and resources they need to succeed, including access to education, professional development programs, and leadership opportunities. The Royal must mentor the Servants and identify potential leaders within the workforce, helping them climb the ladder of success. The King must set the vision for these opportunities and ensure that the organization's policies, compensation structures, and cultural practices align with these goals.

The future of the kingdom lies in breaking down the barriers that limit upward mobility, providing individuals with the opportunities and support they need to rise and contribute to the kingdom's success.

A Legacy for Future Generations: Passing on Lessons Learned

The true legacy of any kingdom is not just its wealth or power—it is the knowledge, wisdom, and values that are passed down to future generations. For a kingdom to thrive for generations, it must ensure that the lessons learned by the King, the Royal, and the Servants are shared and passed on. This means creating systems that allow knowledge transfer, mentorship, and the continuation of the kingdom's core values.

The King must recognize that their legacy is shaped by their ability to teach, mentor, and inspire future leaders. The Royal must focus on creating a culture of learning, where knowledge is shared openly and where everyone in the organization has access to the tools they need to succeed. The Servants, too, must embrace the role of knowledge transfer, sharing their experiences and insights with others to help future generations rise within the kingdom.

A legacy is also about creating a sense of responsibility—to the community, to the environment, and to society as a whole. The future of the kingdom must be built on ethical decision-making, sustainability, and social responsibility. The King, the Royal, and the Servants must understand that their actions today will impact future generations, and they must work together to build a kingdom that is not only prosperous but also responsible and ethical.

Conclusion: Building a Lasting Legacy for Generations

The future of the kingdom depends on its ability to evolve, adapt, and create opportunities for all roles. The King, Royal, and Servants must work together to ensure that the kingdom remains relevant in an ever-changing world. By fostering collaboration, communication, and mutual respect, the kingdom can thrive in the future. The key to building a lasting legacy is ensuring that the lessons learned from past successes and failures are passed down, creating a foundation that allows future generations to build on the kingdom's success. Through innovation, education, and shared responsibility, the kingdom can continue to grow, adapt, and provide opportunities for all its members, ensuring prosperity for generations to come.

Conclusion

As we've explored throughout this book, the roles of King, Royal, and Servant are not isolated—they are interdependent and essential to the functioning of any thriving kingdom. Each role has its place in the ecosystem of the organization, and when they work together in harmony, they create an environment where success is shared, prosperity is attainable, and opportunities for growth are endless. The King, Royal, and Servant each contribute to the kingdom's economy in their own unique way, and it is through collaboration, mutual respect, and understanding that the kingdom flourishes.

The King, as the visionary and leader, is responsible for setting the direction and ensuring the organization grows and evolves to meet future challenges. Their wealth and success are intrinsically tied to the prosperity of the kingdom, but the true measure of a King's greatness lies not in personal gain but in the lasting impact they leave behind—a legacy that ensures the organization continues to thrive for generations. Through investments in their people and creating systems that support upward mobility, the King can ensure that their kingdom remains a place of opportunity and growth, where every role, from the Royal to the Servant, can contribute to and benefit from success.

The Royal, positioned as the key implementer of the King's vision, plays a crucial role in translating big ideas into everyday action. But the Royal's role goes beyond just managing the business; they are the bridge between the King's dreams and the Servants' hard work. They must create an environment where individuals feel supported, valued, and empowered to reach their full potential. A Royal who embraces mentorship, adapts to change, and drives innovation can help build a kingdom that not only survives but thrives.

For the Servant, the journey is one of overcoming financial struggles and building a path to upward mobility. While often the most vulnerable in the economic hierarchy, the Servant is not without hope. The key to breaking the cycle of financial hardship lies in education, self-improvement, networking, and developing the skills necessary to rise. The Servant, through dedication and resilience, can move from financial instability to financial freedom, contributing meaningfully to the kingdom's success.

A kingdom's future depends on the interdependence of these roles and the shared responsibility of creating a balanced, sustainable economy. As each individual —whether King, Royal, or Servant—supports the success of the others, the kingdom becomes a place where all can thrive. Unity, collaboration, and communication are essential to this harmony, and when each person is committed to the greater good, the organization flourishes.

As I reflect on the lessons shared throughout this book, I cannot help but acknowledge the profound impact that Mark, the owner of the local gas station chain, has had on my thinking and life. Our conversation years ago, when I asked him why he hadn't promoted a regular cashier to manager, introduced me to the powerful concept of the King, Royal, and Servant. Mark's wisdom and insight into the interconnectedness of these roles reshaped my understanding of business and leadership. It was a pivotal moment that inspired me to think beyond wealth accumulation and consider the broader purpose of building an organization that benefits everyone involved.

Mark's influence taught me that true leadership isn't about control or dominance—it's about collaboration, mentorship, and creating opportunities for others to succeed. He showed me the importance of investing in people and ensuring that every individual, regardless of their role, has the chance to grow, contribute, and thrive. Through his example, I learned that a kingdom's strength lies not in the power of one, but in the unity and success of all.

As I look toward the future, I am committed to carrying forward the lessons learned from Mark and the principles explored in this book. The future of any kingdom, including our own, depends on how we evolve, adapt, and work together. We must create a legacy built on unity, collaboration, and shared success, where the King, the Royal, and the Servants are empowered to reach their fullest potential. The journey is long, but it is one that promises growth, opportunity, and a lasting impact—for ourselves, for our organizations, and for future generations.

In the end, a kingdom's legacy is not just about wealth—it's about creating a place where every role is respected, every individual has the opportunity to thrive, and the success of the organization is shared by all. Through mutual support, a commitment to growth, and a vision for the future, we can build a kingdom that stands the test of time—a kingdom that creates prosperity, opportunity, and lasting value for generations to come.

www.ingramcontent.com/pod-product-compliance
Lightning Source LLC
Chambersburg PA
CBHW071542220526
45469CB00003B/894